The Bright Nails
Scattered on the Ground

Also by Allen Grossman

A Harlot's Hire (1961)

The Recluse (1965)

And the Dew Lay All Night Upon My Branch (1973)

The Woman on the Bridge Over the Chicago River (1979)

Against Our Vanishing: Winter Conversations with Allen Grossman on the Theory and Practice of Poetry, Conducted and Edited by Mark Halliday (Rowan Tree Press, 1981)

Of the Great House: A Book of Poems (1982)

The Bright Nails Scattered on the Ground

love poems

ALLEN GROSSMAN

A New Directions Book

Grateful acknowledgment is made to the editors and publishers of various
magazines and books in which some of the poems in this volume originally
appeared: *The Graham House Review, Grand Street, New Directions in
Prose and Poetry, The Yale Review.*

Parts of this book were written with assistance of grants from the John Simon
Guggenheim Memorial Foundation and the National Endowment for the Arts.

Manufactured in the United States of America
First published as New Directions Paperbook 615 in 1986
Published simultaneously in Canada by Penguin Books Canada Limited

Library of Congress Cataloging-in-Publication Data
Grossman, Allen R., 1932-
    The bright nails scattered on the ground.
    (A New Directions Book)
    I. Title.
PS3557.R67B7   1986   811'.54   85-31078
ISBN 0-8112-0976-8 (pbk.)

New Directions Books are published for James Laughlin
by New Directions Publishing Corporation,
80 Eighth Avenue, New York 10011

Contents

Weiter noch zieht es den Jüngling; vielleich dass er eine junge
Klage liebt . . . Hinter ihr her kommt er in Wiesen. Sie sagt:
—Weit. Wir wohnen dort draussen . . . Wo? Und der Jüngling
Folgt.

The young man walks farther on. Perhaps he is in love with a young
Lament . . . He follows after her into the meadows. She says:
—*Far. We live out there* . . . Where? And the young man
Follows.

Rainer Maria Rilke, Duino Elegies

The Bright Nails
Scattered on the Ground

1

The Song of the Lord

THE SONG OF THE LORD

There is a table bountifully spread.

In the full sunlight when there is no cloud
And under cloudy skies,
And when there are no stars and when the stars
Distill the time,

           the table stands in a field.
It is late morning and the service shines.
The guests have wandered from the company.
The Lord is alone.

           It is good to hear
The voice of the Lord at rest in his solitude.

The guests have wandered from the table set,

But they hear the voice of the Lord at rest:

The song of the Lord in solitude goes up,
Ten times enfolded, blue, and saturate
With law to the heavens at noon of gaze,
And down among the graves and the darker animals.
The song of the Lord indicates the dust
Of the roadway, the random hammer of the sea,
The riddled vase of mind and mind's dependencies

And pain lost otherwise and lost in this.

The voice of the Lord opens the gates of day.
Air streams through our eyes and brushes the pupils

Streams through our eyes and this is how we see.

THE WORK

A great light is the man who knows the woman he loves

A great light is the woman who knows the man she loves

And carries the light into room after room arousing
The sleepers and looking hard into the face of each
And then sends them asleep again with a kiss
Or a whole night of love

      and goes on and on until
The man and woman who carry the great lights of the
Knowledge of the one lover enter the room

        toward which
Their light is sent and fit the one and the other torch
In a high candelabrum and there is such light
That children leap up

     unless the sea swallow them
In the crossing or hatred or war against which do not
Pray only but be vigilant and set your hand to the work.

THE HOUSE OF WATER

One voice thunders above the rest—the ocean.

Great heroes are the seafarers with their harp-
Like shipping in charge. And great are the swimmers,
Who give and take. And the prophet fishermen,
Who cast and retrieve. But we are summoned
By thunder from walking the common shore
Into the house of water,

                           under the many
Voices and the harp-like shipping, the swimmers,
And the prophet fishermen harassing
The light.

Walk with me from the shore into the ocean—

To the cold first water, which makes the foot
Mute and conscious. With the conscious foot
Walk on toward the empty horizon,
Down through the oak and the sharp, bright grasses,
Across the strewn blue detritus and the shaken sand,
And the wrack—like two waters, murmuring
And falling astonished from separate mountains.
Under the immense instrument of the music
That thunders above us, go to be married
In the one voice that receives all earth.

And you say to me, "It is a dark place, Allen"
And I say, "This is the house of water—
Vacant except for soundless springs
Far, far away."
"So we must labor alone," you say, "like men
At war on the dark floor of water's house."
And we do mortal struggle with one another there,

Until we are as water is in water. Then
I say, "Sister," and you say to me, "My brother,"
And the great instrument of music above us
Changes its note,

                              and our own voices enter
Into the chains of the same work of love
And we are carried up

                              heavier in the air.
As our talk again divides into two waters
—The voice of a man and the voice of a woman—

We walk backward upstream into the mountains.

THE GATE

The day shrieks open—like an ancient gate,
Turning on a bronze post, socketed in stone.
And then shrieks shut, turning in the same
Stone. And the dead bolt of the dark is shot.
Someway from the gate, at the edge of a road,
Is an oak. On the road men and women pass,
Carrying things, leading animals.
Above the road, the oak tree hangs out one
Fear branch, heavy and black. There is no city.
Only the gate, the road, the night, the oak
Tormented by the weight of its one limb,
And men and women carrying this and that,
Leading animals. In the day the men
And women see many things. . . .
At night the men and women see one thing.

What do the men and women see by day?
They look down, and they see the road they walk.
Whether they walk toward the gate or away,
Or linger in the light, they see the road.
When they look at one another, they see
The one body of each of them that stands,
As it were, in the open gate of light.
There is no city of light, only light.
The fear-branch of the oak casts down its shadow
In the road they walk, as if it fell
All day into the dark.

At night, the men and women of the road
Look up. They all look up, in the dark,
And see the sky.
They have set down the things they carried.
The animals sleep in the road at their feet.
They do not remember the gate. They do
Not prophesy the light. They see one thing:
The sky, the sky, the sky, the sky, the sky.

A MAN AND WOMAN

I. THE MAN

My sex is like a legend never told
Out to the end where surely there is homecoming,
A feast, and deep sleep after the many islands—
Some rich in remembering, and others mere
Desolate atolls of loss and loathing where
The unrelenting life of the depths transpires
In the air—and landfalls that break the heart
With strangely guarded wealth and vanishing welcome.

But in my time with you I have been born
To a better infancy in your arms,
And the sexual strength of my body, grown
Toward the greeting of its youth in you,
Has swelled to flourishing, though late—and now
Leans toward the long free telling to the end.

II. THE WOMAN

Behind the wall where the Resistance was shot
Was a wild field where I went to be free.
And I walked the streets of Antwerp and Prague,
And I lay down on the breasts of Provence
Because I found no man to love in whom
There was kindness. And I gave many to drink
From the well of my sex but they gave me
Pain for my love and I fled to America.

Had we met in another place, we would
Not have known one another. Wandering
Has brought us from the ends of the earth
To sit down at this table in the light.
Drink from the cold well of my sex, dear brother
—And the blue tent of kindness cover us over.

8

WILLOW BALLAD

I

First teacher of kindness—the willow tree of the lake
Made a lap for the children, and they came up,
And among them I,
To the throne of her bosom, by a low stair—
From which reached out the soaring comfort of her limbs.
And many had come to this world's best place,
And made the bark smooth and human-warm,
An easy climb;
But hard, hard it was to ascend from there
Into the powers of the air.

II

When I was a child, the willow tree of the lake
Bent over the water and saw herself,
Like a mother who gazes in a mirror and gives
Her breast to a child that does not wake.
Sometimes a flaw of the wind, or a boat with its oars,
Wrinkled the mirror which the deep peace
Of the lake restores.
And the child dreams of the peace of the lake
Whither at the end of day the water
Draws the picture of the willow-mother down
Among all the poet images.

III

Then I was a boy, with slippery shoes, who fell
Awake and longed to climb

The leaf-streaming limbs of the willow tree
To the highest bough, that nobody knows,
And sit alone in the sky
In the treasury of the snows;
And see from above in the lake below
The face of the mother as she sees herself.
But the climb was too hard. And a dizzy fear
Drove me out of the air,

IV

Who afterward came as a youth in the night
To the cross of her limbs under the moon,
And lay down on the throne
With my sex in my hand—a mortal charge—
Which the moon drew up and the winds made large
With their subtle tongues;
And the broken water-lights of the mind enraged.
And her limbs received the sperm of my youth
From the hand of my loneliness
Under the moon which made the world gray.
And I dressed with loathing, and ran away

V

And was gone a long time. But the willow, which is
A short-lived tree
And was old when it first made a lap for me
As a mother is to a son, withdrew herself
To the picture she made in the peace of the lake,
And disappeared. And nothing is left in its space
By day or by night but the air and the light:
A great expectancy in a leaf-strewn hollow.

It is as I feared. There is no face;
And I cannot follow.

VI

Now on the scaffold of my middle life,
How the willow was overthrown I see:
It was a night of storm, and a loathsome thing
Was laboring out
From the cross of her limbs I had sown
With my sperm under the moon.
The soaring limbs lie broken on the ground,
That were so kind; and the worm, begotten on a mother
By her son, triumphs and looks about.
As for the throne, a man who came with a knife
Cut it up and carried it away.

VII

And so I made this willow-ballad of the cold storm
And the man with the knife
As a memorial of the kindness of the willow,
And to prolong its life among the diminished
Treasures of expectancy. I have not found
My mother's picture in the end, which was drawn down;
But from the water-mirror on which she gazed
Has come the image of another, for whose sake
I bless the worm
Upon the ground beside the lake.

A SHORT WALK

alma Venus
     Lucretius

Standing in the road and nobody calling,
After morning rain, and before the rains
Of April noon and April afternoon
And evening. On my right, is the house where
I live. On my left, is the house where
I do not live. The road behind I have
Gone over, and the road before I have
Also gone over, and above is nothing,
And beneath my feet is the earth. —A destruction

Has befallen here among depthless pools.

It is equal whether I stay or go.
Nobody is calling. I can hear sounds,
But they are not calling: there are birds—
The birds of April—but they do not call;
And the winds departing that left the early rain
I hear, and the winds approaching with the rains
Of noon and April afternoon; and the sound
Of the one thing that can happen on this earth
Gathering to take effect. . .

What am I doing now? I begin the walking.

Here are white flakes, veined ash—I think—driven down
From the cold tower of ash, the flowering dogwood,
Luminous ruin. Nearby, loiters the cherry tree,
A sleepy shepherd with his flute in hand strayed
From the meadow, adorned with flowers of his song.
Alma, alma, is it a dream? Is it
Even a dream? The being that has gone through
All its growth—neither the wise (tower
Of ash) nor the beautiful!

In the daybook, mark this day for a *feria*—

A destruction has set me free. I hear my voice
Say, "No!"—the first truth. I can hardly move
The leaden cape of the air. On the right,
At the turning—a sill of death, the silent
Drawing into vacancy. That way
Everything is bright because it is falling,
Brighter than diamond, than wedding stone.
The left is my way to the human end,
The open, whither no one is calling.

Where the open is, there the festival

Never falters on the shores of the sky.
I rose from my chair, hearing no calling,
And walked out on the rain-wet road, and turned
At the drawing of the diamond stone,
And threw off the leaden cape of the air. . . .
To the greater poet remains the song!
The being that has gone through all its growth
Neither the wise, nor yet the beautiful.
For the phoebe was heard again this year

In April but did not nest in the garden.

—Only a few things happen to a man,
And he does not know another thing. But
They are what he knows for sure. It is like
A short walk to the human end alone, seeing
The one thing that can happen on this earth,
And hearing the rain of April afternoon
Come on, and the midsummer rains. And then
The rains of Autumn and the coming of the snow.
And then—*alma, alma*—the poem of the snow.

A CONVERSATION

I. THE MOON

While you were grieving, I was walking under the stars.

"Are there stars, Allen?" There *are* stars, Luce. It is
Bitter you should grieve

                         after love; and I walk out
With odors of your body on my body among the winds
Of August, and see the stars.

                        "There are many worlds on earth,
Allen. Yours is one, and mine another one

                             —no matter
How close."

        There are many worlds in the heavens, Luce;
And the eyes with which I see them are serene, and lifted
Up toward inextinguishable lights.

                     "Allen, nothing above
Restores a mortal loss: the haunted childhood of the mind
In which, night after night unceasingly, a phantom family
Spreads the tables of the living with empty places
For the unreturning dead."

Under my body, sister, be consoled; and in my eyes.

"I cannot be consoled. You are too young. Look up!
Only grief is—
The widow soul who wanders the mortuary sky
Alone."

II. LUCE'S SONG

Grief is an irresistible wave
    Higher than the stars.

Its springs were before the world.
    Its stream never ceases.

Age after age mothers and lovers
    Weep without sound.

Darkness when the wave is past
    Wastes the human shore.

AT THE SHORE

On the *plage* the mothers make paper flowers,
And the children buy them with North Sea shells.

What do the children do with the paper flowers
The mothers make? They plant them in the sand

And the North Sea wave waters them with storms.
Who rests assured

                    in the house of the senses?
It is all restless turning and vanishing.

Dreams tire the mind, exhaust the heart of
The sleepers—many dreams.

                        Therefore I say
To you up there who are not in this with me
You who do not know me except for this,
The man or woman awakens exhausted
At the heart.

            I cannot imagine the dead
In ecstasy. I do often imagine
The dead in torment,

                 and the blue dome of
The house where the order is written.

THE KNIFE

Perhaps for others knowledge can come slowly
In the leisure and happiness of casual disclosures,
As one might learn without need the name of a flower
That has a use,
Or how to find the path through to the waterfall;
But for us the whole story of each of us down to
Nakedness must be told out quickly,
Because the overpowering phantoms stand in awe
Only of the meticulous telling of the tale.

(Come to me, dear Luce; your brother is waiting.)

And I have thought, at times, that no two persons ever
Knew one another so well as we, and that we had broken
The mortal barrier that divides one friend's mind
From the silent mind of his friend;
And I said, "We have overcome the distance between life
And death: we have found the hidden path that leads
From the unappeasable angers of love's distrust
Into the transparent morning of awakening
Both at once in the light."

(Not yet, my brother; I have more to say.)

But I have learned that still from the past and the past's past,
The hurt minds of men and women—unloving fathers
And mothers, and behind them phantom throngs of human
Families in pain stretching to the dark—
Out of remote forest graves send streams of prophetic messengers
To chalk their barbaric grief-marks on this body
Of our love, which we must study after the manner.
Of the severest queen studious by firelight of the face
Of a wandering stranger—
Masked in the history of the world in tears.

(Come to me, dear Luce; your brother is waiting.)

Of what all my life long have I been studious but you?
Yet even the lovers who have known you still lack names,
In whose arms the science of your sex was written
I labor at alone—late walking
In the tragic night-theater of the shadows and the stars:
And this is your picture as a girl in the wind
Twenty years ago,
Radiant in the bluster on the beach at Herne
Your face to the camera someone holds and the North
Sea behind you rising wave after frozen wave.

(Not yet, my brother; I have more to say.)

But knowledge is also a sadistic blade wielded in anger
Against the body of love; and the end of knowing,
Death's difference driven to the heart.
Can you kiss the face of which the tongue is a flame,
Or the mouth of which the breath is the sea wind?
A man cannot get closer
To a man, or a man to the woman he loves, or a woman
To the woman she loves, or a woman to a man. Yet,
Even in their rooted bed the severest king and queen,
Urgent and cruel, keep on telling

(Come to me, dear Luce; your brother is waiting.)

And do not sleep, for they have taken vows to one another
Against the phantoms, both the messengers from the forest
Graves, and the ghostly picture of autumn at the shore.
Therefore, let us not be proud or afraid,
Although I shall not cross
The plains of Flanders to the beach at Herne where you
Stand smiling at your lover still and behind you the North
Sea rising,
Nor night-walking find the conscious way through death
To the great falls of the mountain.

(Not yet, my brother; I have more to say.)

THE STARE

The whole world cannot comfort you—

Not the visible world extending its ringed hands
And gazing into your eyes like the sun at noon,
Capable lover, or sun at five o'clock,
The husband returning who kisses your face
And in the dark night shows you all his thought;

And not the invisible world that breathes
Quietly on your swollen lips at dawn
And offers you its perfect breasts to suck.
Desire that is greater than the world stares
From your eyes,

                    and I am acquainted with
The earth's rage when women look at the mountains,
And say to one another, "Not enough, not enough,
We will not sleep in this place"—ignorant
What can and cannot be,
And how each thing has a deep-set boundary mark.

—What is left? The work of common life
And long familiarity discovers love.
Do you not see that drops of water falling
On stone after a while penetrate the stone?

The machine of the world will stop, and there
Will be nothing but rain of the *primordia.*

And nothing is indifferent to our claims.

THE WEDDING BAND

Nothing can touch or be touched except bodies:

Hang your sea-drenched garments at the surf-breaking
Shore and they stay wet and get wetter.
Carry them into the sun, and they dry.
But how the water got into the shirt
You left on the rocks, or how it was baked
Out in the sun, you cannot see. The facts
Of the body are small.

                After many revolutions
Of the sun a ring on the finger wears
Thin underneath, between the flesh and metal,
As in a long marriage a wedding band
Of gold becomes thin as a silk ribbon.

To the bodies by which nature maintains
The world the eye of man is blind.

IN RUIN'S HOUSE

What will become of us? "I do not know."

When you were born, I was thirteen.
The war, remote from me, was your weird cradle
Shaken from the skirts of ruin's empire.
Around your cradle the near faces were
Pale with loss, the houses of your infancy
Blown through with ghosts, and men and women seeking
The destinies of ghosts. Love was uncertain
Of the ground.

        My desire was born when you were
Born, and journeyed on the same uncertain ground,
Although remote, until we came
In one another's arms to the one question:
Whether to trust or die.

           "A ghost,
My brother, is a passion without a world,
A *revenant* returning in rage and pain
From the very shallow grave of the earth
Crazed with desire,
Whose caresses are the winds, and strengthless
Crying out for love a rainy language of
The East no one remembers here more than
The wind.

        In ruin's empire love chooses
Its vows in solitude by its own light
And lies down on the shaken ground in mind;
And being motherless it has no songs,
And fatherless no witnessing. What could
I learn of trust in ruin's house, where came
And went only returning spirits who are
Never kind? I do not trust you, Allen.

What will become of us?"

                 —In 1944 I heard
On the radio a story of two lovers
Who were beautiful,
Whose perfect love and trust were envied
By an intimate, crazed demon of the war
And times and of my dreams. And he imprisoned
Them in ruin's house. And having failed to
Make the one believe the other's infidelity
He cut away their beauty with some knives
Leaving only mind,
On which uncertain ground he put again
To those changed lovers in a room his question
"Do you still love?"

               They were no longer human
To the eye
But they could see. And also they could speak,
Though what they said I cannot now remember.

They did not die.

"What will become of us?" I do not know.

POLAND OF DEATH (I)

I hear my father underground scratching with a nail. And I say,
"Father, here is a word." He says, "It does not help. I am
Scratching my way with a nail ever since you dug me down
In the grave, and I have not yet come to Poland of death."
And I hear my mother saying, "Sing me something about the
Forest primeval." So I say, "Mother, here is a story."
And she says, "I have a pain in the blind eye, the left one
Which is dead."

           I hear my father scratching with a nail again,
And I offer him the words of a song, first one word and then
Another, and he refuses them. He says, "It is not a word," or
"It is just a word," or "It is not what you feel." "What
Do you feel?" Poland of death! Ever since I put my father
In the grave he has been scratching a way, and has not yet
Got under the sea, and mother has a pain in her blind eye.

So I tell her the story of a woman named Irene: How when she
Walked into a hayfield behind her house the animals shrieked.
How when she crossed over to the other side of the field
The clothes in the bluing froze, and all the yeast died
In the potato water. How when she reached the edge of the forest
Everything went up in flames in the farm she had left behind.
Then my father underground says, "Do not be bewildered by
The surfaces. In the depths, everything is law." And I say,
"My true love in the grave-deep forest nation is a forester."
And mother says, "This is the forest primeval." Poland of death!

HER HANDS WITHOUT RINGS

Her hands without rings
Are as beautiful as they are pale and free
And subjects of her own will
A wreath of wreath-makers, and of the crowns
Of life intricate builders
And of the shrouds of death compassionate
Weavers and of the mortal
Covenant severe interpreters.

My hands without rings
On which her bare hands lie are also pale
And all that they remembered
Has now escaped them, wreathed
In new wreathings
They neither give nor take, which was their way,
But rise with hers assured
In a new motion shrouded, crowned, and free.

THE PATIENCE OF THE DARKER LOVER

Though we have had many days, this is the first night of our love.
And we have loved and slept some, and I have dreamed:

            Even in your arms
A darker lover drew my sex away toward cavernous infoldings,
And fear and shame awoke in me because I did not love you
But was devoted to that other one,
More radical, more severe, who was waiting for me in the place
I'd searched for thirty years ago and not found then,
And yet still did wait
Until this first night of our union, this first sleep in your arms.
"I have waited a long time," she said. "Now come to me." And I went,
And you went with me, down into the city of the unlived past.
I said, "It is time to go, my sister, to the darker lover,
For she has waited a long time." And we went to her, you and I,
As if we were one soul in the one body,

          down into the city of the past
Which was not two cities, but the one city of the past we failed
To find before. On the first night of our love she took us—
The lover of the unloved body of my youth—as a woman takes a boy
And draws forth from him the deep first seed of his whole love;
And also the lover of the unloved body of your youth—as a woman
Takes a girl, opening the source of a stream which has never
Yet flowed, that no lover of your youth man or woman had opened.
And I thought, "In the darker lover we have found a stronger bond,
Because she has waited a long time in the city of my unlived past
For me, and in the city of your unlived past for you.

           In one another's
Arms we have gone back, in middle age, and found her on the first night
Of our love." And now I wake, and find *you* in your cotton gown.

NOVEMBER, OR JEALOUSY

I

My sister, my lover,

                what are these tears?
There is a general sadness in the cold,
November rain. Everything is strange, as
In itself it is
Bound to its own or another's interest,
But not to me. The look of the light is turned.
Something makes me ignorant of my life,
And all my words provisional. . . .

            •   •   •

Night after night (all of the nights) my sister
Sleeps with her husband,
And only for certain moments of the day
Is she mine; and so it is with all things—
Faithless, averted earth. And within me
My mind, in the sexual power of another,
Is drawn down by the gravity of his claim.
I shall never be the only lover of
My sister:

            always before my eyes her body
Is naked, as I have known it, on a bed;
And another lover—I recognize—opens her
Legs with his knee, and her sex with his fingers
Which know what they can have. He enters her,
And she is covered from my sight except
A caressing hand along his back, and the gleam
Of a look absorbed in a life that does
Not know me. . . .

It is raining. She has taken in his seed.
What are they doing now in the one bed?
I must simplify my thought—or die.
Surely the intercourse of brother and sister
Is simple as rain falling in water
Is simple utterly

II

My sister, my lover,

We have but one body
Which is not ours, witness of unknown histories—
Like a square tower with an iron door
In a field,
That a man and woman come upon
Walking together in the November rain
And are astonished—and look at one another,
For the first time seeing the strangeness.
"Who made it?" they ask. "How did it come here?"
"What has befallen?"

. . .

And there is no thought so patient, nor look
So long, nor moment of attentiveness forested
So deep in quietness that the loved body
Is really found asleep in its true form;
Or the oak tree of stature startled
From perpetual reverie of her other
Lover, the sun; or the stars of night touched
At the punctual moment of their burning. . . .

And so I look out in tears from the square tower,
Seeing a man and woman find the path

Once more, after their brief astonishment—
And disappear out of the ruined empire
Of November's field.

               Then I look again
And see a crowd of men and women naked
In the smoky rain burning the plague garments
Of memory.

              And for the last time look
And see night rising,
And on the iron door the Winter shuts
A great lock, and sets his ignorant seal . . .

Do not pity me.

III

My sister, my lover,

                  nothing is clean
Against this cold.
In the night air, a vast circling disturbance:
The man and woman, her cries and his dark howling,
Fuck on the unmade bed of Winter wind,
The snow coming on.
And I hear the parent tongues of all my uttering,
Her voice caressing him
(Why does she not cover herself?) and also
The other voice of the dark man which penetrates
Her body and is effective

And weep because the poem is never true.

          •   •   •

No man or woman can utter the true
Poem of a whole life,
Or of a single day, or of one moment
Of the common day;
Yet they walk on, nonetheless, over the rainy,
Promiscuous earth, and do not speak more
Of the unforgettable sentiment—
Of the square tower, or of the dark man
Who will come between them in the end.

And this wild November field, the great world—
Wintering wasps of it, and the lodged grasses,
The rain-worn faces of old nests, clear
Traces of burning, and dark shadow over
Of the cold storm—
Is the only secret of every soul
That lives
And a song to each alone. And consoles
The dead such as are in pain, and rejoices
The dead such as are in joy, and draws on
The dead that have not finished . . .

"It is simple, my brother, as falls this
Voice into your heart
Where only my name is, as water into
Water after rain,
Water dropping, shining, disappearing
Into water."

THE LOCK

Outside the long window of the final poem
—The final poem, like an empty room,

                                   a high

Room of state
Where burns the last of the perpetual fires:
A guttering tongue of the ancient flame,
Or mother-word of the unutterable name
Faltering
In a sealed air, in the night, and unknown weather—

A starved moth of a cry, a moth or cry
Of the soul, or soul

                    batters its wings

Against the transparent gate of the final room
—The dark room of the longest art where burns
Fame of the word that is mother of the cry
And desire of the heart,
The term or a form of the nurturing light
I am drawn to as by fate

Unsealed in a dream when I first remembered
To fly
And felt the lapse and glide and the strong sexual
Rising of sight,
And gazed upon the diminished fields of the world
Without fold or flower, as from the tower
Of an ecstasy. . .

Until night came down bearing laws
And I awoke,

                        and saw far off through the black
The thin flame of the mother-word; and heard
The calling of a name
From the sealed mansion of the book—
The final poem and the adamantine lock.

2

The Man and Woman

A BLUE HERON

. . . a person appeared to him in his sleep, and saluting him by
his name, said, "Caedmon, sing some song to me." He answered,
"I cannot sing; for that was the reason why I left the entertain-
ment, and retired to this place." The other who talked to him
replied, "However, you shall sing."—"What shall I sing?" he
rejoined. "Sing the beginning of created beings," said the other.
—Bede, *Eccles. Hist.*, XXIV

—The poet is dead. This is the forging of his mark:

When I entered the dark wood I cannot remember,
But in dreams I remember. And waking, in my time,
Remember the trick of remembering the dream
Of escape into the dark wood the wrong way through
The gate of light—the dream of which or the imagining
Draws me on through the darkness. And I go inscribing
Memories in the one long page of whatever befalls
The traveler who continues with no other purpose
Than to return to the gate from which he went out
The wrong way, and to enter again in accord with
The true custom of entrance and begin (great verb)
The first day of light and darkness. And I hear a voice
Behind me saying, "There has been silence a long time."
It is the poet's voice, like the bourdon of the grasses, under
All the particular voices, that speaks for them from knowledge
Out of the great stone books in shadowy array like oaks,
A forest as it were of lives—each a stone book, or
Sempiternal diary with a hard lock—that do not open
Any more than stones can open their stubborn hearts.

Where are the lovers, where are all the strong young men?

And now the song of the thrush has at last subsided like
A stopped fountain into the deep pools of its own repose.
Now the black winds of Prime have struck the stone lip of the
    wood,

And time passes as I think. . . . An oracular dream
That takes my form stands at the bed's head of my death
Or dreaming of the gate that flashes from the wood's edge
To the world beyond. I recognize behind me the angelic enemy
Whose voice I speak and hear: "The imagination," he says,
"That reaches to death reaches also to birth. It strays
Backward on and on into the creation—as through a pasture
Gate left open by accident or inadvertence, or some charm
At the moment of the first scattering of all the guests
Across the morning fields toward the dark woods round about—
And then to the beginning, and then back and back. And each
Reaching is a great destruction on the body of the poet
Who desires to be born (such is the oracle of desire)—to turn
The right way through the gate of light before he dies.
The poet alone can undergo the destructions. That is why
He is with you." —There has been silence a long time.

Like a drop of new blood shining on a nail the voice

I speak and hear demands the ending of the poet's story
Of wandering in a dark wood, and the remembering of dreams.
Those who cannot think the thought of God are divided
From themselves, and those who think only the thought of
God are divided from themselves. . . . I feel such great love
Toward the loudest of the strong angels who takes my form
At the bed's head of my dreaming that I do not think I can endure
The ending of the poet's story. Because I cannot choose but
Choose to dwell in the dominion of it, as in the first glance
Of a long love that is conscious all at once, in the beginning,
Of the pouring seas of its final straits and passages, and
The cruel sea birds on it, and the uninhabitable, blue skies
Of its portals and its laws

I TURN FACE TO THE BLANK BLAZON OF HIS FACE

In the hour before dawn, at the edge of the dark wood in trouble,
And cut myself from him one bleeding suture at a time

As from a monstrous shadow into which otherwise all my light
     falls,
And take his sex in my hand and wrestle with him until dawn,
And on his body satisfy my various passions for ignorance,
Shame, and rest. Thus the wrestling trick of remembering the
     dream
Is like the overcoming of God, or it is the kind of thought
Called fire that burns out all the private histories
And the poems of the private histories for they are not
Helpful or true—and the number of them is the same as
The sum of all the worlds that cannot come to pass because
This world has come to pass like a drop of new blood on a nail.
And I know how many destructions are required to make a poem,

Knowing how many destructions are required to make a world:

The one long page of whatever befalls the traveler
For whom the road is open like a virgin scroll or a fan
As he turns for the first time the right way through the gate
Into the world of light and darkness, and beholds the Gothic
Thunderheads of an afternoon in August blow up over the Vlatava
Painting earth with the particular darkness of the city of Prague—
The unmistakable stain of the first darkness that was before
The beginning of created beings—its own black wreath.
The poet has killed the poet, and through the air, like ghosts
Of the dead, or unborn spirits, the plumed seed of the Cotton-
Woods of Prague are driven to the ground or into the river.
This is the beginning and the end to which the imagination
     comes.
This is the birth of the world out of the lure of the voice.
The men and women of Prague, that the afternoon brought forth,
Take shelter like enraptured readers of a great, new witness
Among the oaks of the river islands. It is better, I see now,
That the poem should not always come out well—as when the
Children are at their music and the music wavers and complains.
In the necropolis of the city of Prague there is also darkness

Until the sun makes pale the flames of the cineraria.

It seems in the end the wood has never been silent,
Or the great books closed that stand in shadowy array
Like oaks—each with a stone of witness at its stubborn heart.
Let us return to the entertainment. There are always many
Particular voices: as from the point of view of the darkness
There is no light, and from the point of view of the living
There is no death, and from the point of view of the Creation
There is no God, and from the point of view of the dead
There is no life, and from the point of view of the light
There is no darkness or wandering and never has been any.
What shall I sing? The storm wind has gone over the meadow
Of created beings and in the sky there hangs the bright
Bow of the beginning, or great weapon of the hero lately put
    aside
After the long wars of men and gods—a sign of covenant
To the world that everything is born that is to be born.
Out of the deep pool of its own repose which is its music
The thrush flies up restored. What shall I sing to you now?
Not the fame of destructions but remembrance, and not
    remembrance.
Because the last word of the story is not by the poet.

Why do you spare, hammer that is always rising, now even now?

                        •   •   •

Beyond the meadow flow the water meadows, and beyond
The water meadows the waters of the stream—diminished
At this season of the year, a dry August, but now more
Full of light and darkness than the evening sky. Westward,
Beyond the meadows and the stream are the darkening hills.
Behind the hills the sun of the world sets out of sight—diffusing
A luminous low regard. Whatever is stands, as it were,
In the gates of light and darkness. On the water meadows
Are millions of lilies (they are not numerous, they abound),
And on a raised bank, men and women. They do not dream,
They do not wander in their dream. They look at the lilies.

They come to look, and as the light grows less and less they fall
To talk of how they went out into light and now they pass the
   gate
Again to darkness, according to the laws of the gate, seeing
The waters drawing down like the first waters of the world,
And among the lilies (look! look there!) a great blue heron—
He who survives the destruction of all the worlds, and is
In every world the same—like a master's stroke in a cruel tint
On the darkening stream, alien and final—the destroyer's mark.

O Cantor Apollo, take in hand the work of the holy world.

EURYDICE, OR THE THIRD REICH OF DREAMS

Wir Gewaltsamen, wir währen länger.
Aber *wann,* in welchem aller Leben,
sind wir endlich offen und Empfänger.

We have the power, we last longer.
But *when,* in which one of all our lives,
Are we, finally, open and found?

—Rilke, *Die Sonette an Orpheus,* Zweiter Teil, 5.

Aëllo the wide woman with fish eyes
Is seated before the door of her house.
She is bright as dark is bright. Her hair
Is tied back. Her large breasts are concealed.
She does not wear black but white as white
Is black. I stand before her and she makes
Love to me. Her legs are closed but she
Draws me through her vagina into her womb.
She teaches me I do not know what . . .
She says, YOUR GUILT IS UNDENIABLE.

•

This is not to be sent.—I am calling you from so far. Please hear me under all the noise. I am awake now. I want no more dreams tonight. Between my bed, which fills almost the whole room, and the window is a small card table at which I am writing to you, and a bookcase full of the weepiest books—*Das Drittes Reich des Traums* by Charlotte Beradt, *Se ressaisir ou disparaître* by Isaac Pugatsch, *Encore un effort* by General Robert Close, *The Black Book of Prague* . . .

—I had to stop for a little while. I have found one book here—a new one—which enumerates each convoy from this city, every name and the circumstances of death as

they are known, the exact number of people gassed on arrival—
boys, girls, men, women—the number of people killed later, and
the survivors. Allen, it is one thing to argue from the point of
view of the living and rant and rave, but then there is the side of
the faces in this book—the side of the dead!

I am sure there is
also a book of my own death somewhere, but I do not know who
has it. If you could find it, you would see that it is not like a
poem or a letter—it is more like an August storm that blows up
over the castle and the river, and fills the air of afternoon with
sudden darkness and the plumed seeds of the cottonwoods and
dust, and then passes over the city like waking or sleep. You
would see that it has nothing to do with destructions, or with the
beginning or the end.

.

—For who shall say, as between the man and the woman,
Which is the most delighted in love? Or as between
The new dead in the moment after death and the unborn
In the moment before birth, which is summoned to
The severest judgment? Or as between brother and brother,
Or sister and her sister, or a sister and her brother,
Or friend and dear friend, which will answer for both of them
And for the common world? Go and ask the flowers
Because thought is like the flowers, and of two kinds:
There are the flowers near to me that close in the night
—Such as the outlandish lily that is my particular
Passion, or the anemone—and make a holy difference
Between night and day, sisters confident of memory.
But other flowers keep open to the rains of the moon
Like men and women intending to be present at the inter-
Course of their own death—as the night-blooming *cereus*
That blossoms at the hour prophetic Job called pain,
And knows the profane horror of the millennium;
Or the common marigold—*souci des marais*—

Flower of the marshes raped night after night by the trained
Dogs of the torturer and the torturer's question.

•

My dearest, we have a duty *not to remain in the aftermath of things.*

I read just now, in Charlotte Beradt's book, of a doctor who
dreamed—in 1934, after one year of life in the Third Reich—that
the walls of his room had disappeared and as far as the eye could
see no apartments had any walls. And then in his dream the doc-
tor heard a voice on a loudspeaker, "According to the decree of
the 17th of this month on the Abolition of Walls. . . ." I think
it must be either Heaven *or Hell* where there are no walls!

—In the book of convoys, the new one I mentioned to you, are
photos of children holding the hands of mothers and walking the
same streets I walk, with sight of the familiar trolley in the back-
ground. In one picture is a young boy with an intelligent look
who stares in a very serious way at the camera. Whether he
knows something the others do not, of course I cannot tell . . .

•

But we are guided in these matters by
A spirit of our kind—whose eyes are averted,
Whose color is a blue of the bland mortal power,
A mother of light who gives us all her face
In whose domain we are—in love—unknown,
And subjects of the whitest languages
Wherein the light discourses generously
Of her children who have in her no name—
Translator snows.
Left to themselves all things tend toward this place,
A visionary dome, or Tivoli with stars inside
And one gigantic wheel, a *Rieserad*
On which the lighted coaches slowly turn. . . .

There was a night, my brother, when mother came
Wrapped in a mantle like a Summer storm,
After a ball, with sequins in her hair
And the outer air, and whispered to each of us,
"My dear"—though I was here, and you elsewhere
In another time. Help me to keep
Her holy, in whom we met.
The walls of the world have been abolished by decree—
It is the one new fact of history
That nothing is holy, now, because there is no place:
The pallid angels of the Nations in their killing clothes
Preside
With female courtesy at the abolition
Of the face;
And the trained dogs of the moon have slipped
The leash and hunt us through the *Buchenwald*
Or immemorial beech forest of the book
And all the fragrant paths lead to a lock.
By their nature men desire to know the end
And the beginning, and thus they violate
The nurseries of the snow. . . .
If you come for me, you must avert your eyes.
You must forget my body and my name,
Because I speak another language
In which nothing you can say is true, nothing the same.
There are no spirits and there cannot be—
Just the seeds of the world—and the flowing leaf—
Dropping one after one into the bed of the Spring.
—I write to you in English to be safe.

•

I have attempted to look away from the paper, and beyond the book of names and faces, in this room which is now very empty. I shall soon stop, and—because I have not gone mad with fear— try to sleep and try not to dream.

I want no dreams tonight. Last night I dreamt that posters had been set up on every corner proclaiming in white letters on a black background the twenty words people are not allowed to say. The first was "Lord." The last was "I." The others I cannot remember. But tonight, please, no dreams.

•

The strangest of my many bodies lies awake in the night.
Above me is a gate and in it the weary angel of the gate
—Emptiness of a body without the passion of the ghost,
The unbodied substance of him like cords blowing in another
    air—
Appointed to stand undying at a threadlike border as of
Another mind, where knowledge of the world comes to an end,
And thought comes to the end and stops. He holds two books:
With his thin left hand he shows me the book of the wound;
With his right, the book of the knife. At first the wound
Is beautiful like a new friend or an astonishing ornament.
But soon it becomes familiar and cruel with the cruelty
Of a frightened woman or a beaten child grown dark and
    cunning
With malice and secrecy. After that, it begins to speak sentences.
And, finally, it makes its mark. Thus, I finish reading in
The book of the wound and turned to my left side where the
    angel
Of the gate shows me the book of the knife—his voice like
A tree with wind in it, his whole body more and more the sub-
Stance of morning wind: "Now the knife works without the
    hand.
In the cities of man it works on the bodies of the citizens.
It works only on the flesh of men and women. It has no destiny
Toward wood or stone." He ceased and disappeared, leaving me
The two books of my life, the book of the wound and the other
Book of the knife. In the strangest of my many bodies I arise,
And cross the threadlike border of another mind, and wake.

•

Midnight here. I shall mail this letter in the morning with some misgiving. What I feel is a new thing for me, rather passionless—neither anger, nor resentment, nor painful love, a sense of the others as *so other* that only the calmest affection is elicited, *a very white sort of compassion.*

In Vienna once—in the old days, after the war—I crossed over from the Lueger-Ring to Freud's apartment at 19 Berggasse to see the famous *Abhandlungzimmer,* but it was empty—all the images, and pain, and labor at thought and writing leaving not even a stain in the air. Only light was left after all the destructions—meticulous and absorbed—neither adding nor taking away.

But there was the shadow of an old man lingering in the room, exhausted and appalled by the realization that everything he knows is true, everything everybody knows is true. . . . Why should I insist on love? Why should I *insist!*

•

Dearest, I am captive in a House where dark
Is light, governed by an inconsolable queen
With whom I am in love—Aëllo, hypnotic
Nurse. She teaches me the lure of the source,
And the terror of despotic memory.
If you do not come for me, I shall remain
Naked, her sexual slave, and eat dust.
She rules *all worlds that cannot be*—by force.
But if you *do* come—do not look at me—
Do not touch me—*do not say my name.* . . .

3
Lecture of Light

AUGUST OF THE PERSEIDS

ultima multis

Come with me on my walk tonight, my phantom
Sister—Luce, or the light. It is high summer.
The hour is late. The night is dark. Listen!
There is a bird of few notes who keeps on
Through every hour of the darkness.

It is a quiet world. The negligent villas

Lie open to the air like naked sleepers,
Half-awake, who stir a little in the doom-
Light of the night lamp, and call out a name
Again, and then again;
And I have heard the delicate chiming of
A sweet-voiced clock strike punctually
The latest hour from the darkest room.

Visit me. And I will show you where the
Blind fountain underneath the hill threads patiently
The needle's eye of sight and through the fustian
Of the night draws out unerringly
A brilliant line;
And where a fluent thrush from the high pines
On the side-hill enlarges all the worlds.

Here is the neighborhood where I walk,
Under the moon in August of the Perseids.

WAKING

a poem mentioning the name of Maggie Cooks

"For God's sake look after our people."—Scott, March 23, 1912

I

To know. What is it?

　　　　　—At midday, or a little after,

In the midwinter garden,

　　　　　　　　the noon sun brightens the face
Of the garden stone—its hollows and crevasses, its habitable
Upland fields and dizzying unwalkable fells. The weird Peruvian
Alp of a mountain wilderness brightens for the one moment of
The brightening light,

　　　　　　　　an ancient and enduring summer wilderness
On the face of the winter stone in warm, wet February,
The stone of my garden.

　　　　　—This is not my right life.

And then the February sun said many other sentences, as it were
In haste, to the end of the lecture of the light.

II

　　　　　　　　Cloud of winter's storm,
I know three things:

　　　　　—The one page given me to keep is lost,

That now the death-voice of the dark demands; and it is not
To be found on earth or in heaven.

                            —The one choice exacted,
I cannot perform; and love does not exonerate. And now the death-
Cloud of winter storm makes light less and less.

                            —The one face,
The wanting which makes death in life for me, has not been born;
And I have no song to open the gates of Hell.

                            But think of the dead
Girl, Maggie Cooks. Think of her! She took poison, wrapped an electric
Blanket around her body, and died. The blanket that warmed
And comforted her body rotted her

                      to unrecognizability,

Made her flesh flow. —*Woe to the man who is silent about you!*

III

                        What is, then? What is it?

A woman came to me and said:

                      "Not long before my wedding I dreamed
I lay in my grave. When the first dust was thrown down on my face,
I felt sharp pain;

                and it came to me in my dream that all the dead
Feel such pain when the first dust of burial is thrown down
On their faces."

           What is it? I so want to know.

                                  49

                                        —Any one who looks
Can see images and films thrown off from the outermost surfaces
Of things, bitter spray of the headlands that flits through air,
Hither and thither

                    like torn nets, as wood throws off smoke, as
Cicalas their thin coats in summer. Knowledge is common as light.
But a man cannot teach it to a man, nor an angel to an angel, nor
An angel to a man—

                    white writing from a white hand fallen

In a page of snow.

IV

On our gardens the black cloud of winter lays lock and shadow,
And on the white body of the lady of the garden

                                        the whole truth
Of time: *The night cometh when no man can work.* And of the ones
who go out to the work and return,

                            coming home along their winter
Track in the howling summer of impassable ice when the white
Body of the lady of the garden light

                            begins to turn and sigh,
In their blinded eyes "a comfortable blue look"; and also of
The others who go out and do not return

                            the poem is the same:
After the horror of the pole, a bare flat place planted with a
Black flag,

THE TREE OF KNOWLEDGE DEAD;

                                    and after the long summer
Waking, as the January sun invisible to the eyes burns its mark in
Through the closed eyelids of the late sleeper,

                                        the eye of the mind
Flutters, and then opens. What the dreamers feared in their dreams,
The waking mind finds true.

                    (*For God's sake look after our people.*)

Light has more to say.

THE JEW'S DAUGHTER

If I have misunderstood *this,* I have mis-
Understood everything! —I say to you,
I have misunderstood it all. But I
Have not mistaken this misunderstanding,
Because I dreamed a true dream. This is
The dream

         —at the dark edge of a darker falls,
In the moment when the fall seems to stop,
The moment of recovery and transparence
Before it drops into the first abyss,
The first of many soundless cataracts,
Each under each, down which the world pours
Like rivers of water to the darkest dark

I enter a dream theater—the truth shop

Or *Wunderkammer* of our common life
In the transparence of the last blue wave.
It is a window, lighted from within
By the blue light of the last wave before
The fall, that draws my mind. Jews of the town,
A father and a mother and their one
Child who is a girl, keep the truth shop in
The clear light at the edge of the abyss.
Through them pours the grave waters of the falling
World—lustrous, relentless, cold, quick and still.

They have what I want.

         —a leaf it is, or willow
Rib of a druid fan scribbled with runes,
The last piece of the story. It arouses me
Like a woman. —Then, burdened with the price,
I lean through a crease in the transparent stream

And pay into the hand of the girl my whole
Stake for the poet stick.

                     "Now *read,*" the girl said.

And I translated the words by the blue light
And thus diminished them. It was as if
Great, pilgrim birds—eagle and noble swan—
Sent to the world's center from the darkest limbs
Of earth had lost their way. And the one went
To the mountains, and the other to the deep
Lake of streams to sing and die. —Finally, in the
Theater of dream, I read out the plain words,
And heard the others, dead and unborn, or living
Still reading the same words that concern us
Through all the time the words are true.

                          It was
The identical, birth-blue, starving cry
That worked back across the water to the ship
Of Thamus when he whispered to the shores
At windless Palodes:

             GREAT PAN IS DEAD;

And heard answer him the oldest lamentations,
Not of one person but of many—mingled
With amazement—and not of persons only,
But even the strangled voices of the stones.

Death comes in waves (they cried) *Death comes over us*
In waves, as each day's light is a wave. And
The last wave falling plucks us from the shore.

These words are the dust, O daughter of the Jew.
(The sea is also dust) —This was the dream.

I *must* remember you.

THE STREAM AND THE CANOE

The stream is patient and the canoe that on it
Slides down between the willows and the sky
Is patient and the meadows that the stream covers
And uncovers and colors with the colors of the sky
Now blue now cloudy dark now seeded with the stars
Or with the grasses are patient and breathe slowly
In the confidence of endless time worthy of trust
And the man who steers the canoe and strokes and strokes
Is patient and looks at the willows and the sky
And at the woman in whose trust he comes to know
The patience of the stream
Which rises from a well that has never failed to flow
And descends to a sea that has never failed
To receive its waters that have borne
The canoe that slides without haste in the patience
Of a man who strokes and strokes and a woman at whom
He gazes worthy of trust and there is no diminishing

TO THE TRUMPETS

Perhaps he built a throne—as you would place
A chair for a friend, in a particular light;
But no friend came that day. And so his preparations
Went on and on, becoming more filled with desire
And gold:—more tables of offering, more flags
Of Presence, more scepters of His power laid
Ready for His hand.

               It was all made from trash,
The refuse of government offices, in which he wrapped
Dead lightbulbs and used furniture salvaged,
Or bought. And he wrote prophetic announcements
In watery lavender, like Constantine
Who used no other color.

               I liken the brightness
Of what he made to the desire of the male
That builds up a golden throne for the greater
Poet to come, of whom we say: "Except
The one face there is nothing else." This is
The madness of great love.

               And great love
Changes all things. As once by the sea I went
Down—
The vast sea; and I heard the whole of it
Shift in its bed and rise toward me—grown
From all its throats, and from each throat a thousand
Particular voices, and each voice unanswerable;
And I saw the huge trunk of a dead tree,
Cut elsewhere and heaved up there. And I knew then
For myself—beyond the grim scavage of art—
The desolation of the world and ignorance
Of the heart.

Therefore, call Him the high *hetairos*,
And build up His throne—composed of lost things—
According to the ordinance of knops and flowers:
A chair for the lost one of lost things made,
An imperial friend who comes to sit
In the kingdom of our patience and the courtesy
Of our sexual gold. Hang out more flags,
More and more flags. . . .
Let there be more scepters of His power laid;
Inscribe more glyphs of announcement in watery
Lavender.
Hammer in more gold, more gold, more gold. —Summon

The school children to see what we have done;

But tell them nothing I have just now said.

POLAND OF DEATH (II)

As not in life my father appeared to me
Naked in death and said, "This is my body."
So I undressed and faced him, and we were
Images of one another for he

Appeared to me at the same age I am.

Then he said, "Now I am in Death's country."
And I saw behind him in the dogmatic
Mirror of our death a forest of graves
In morning light. The smoky air was full
Of men and women sweeping the stone sills.
"Since you dug me down in America,"
He said, "I've been scratching a way with a nail,
And now I have come to Poland of Death."

And I saw the keepers of the graves moving
Among the shadows and the lights like lights.

Then he said to me—and not for the first time—
"Give me a word." And again, "Who are you?"
And then, after a long silence, "Write me
The Black Book of the world." And I replied,
"Louis, here is my body." And then one
Of us grew erect, and the cries began—
Like the weak voices of disembodied children
Driving crows from the cornfields.

                                    —He showed me
The severed head of a mother in her tears
Kissing and eating the severed head of a child;
And one familiar spirit like a snarled hank
Of somebody's black hair. And he showed also
A bloody angle of the wires where groans

Of men and women drowned the roar of motors
And mounted to a prophecy. Then he gave me
A sharp look and said, "Thank God, I have no children,"
And ran off with a cry down an alley of
That place like one who remembered suddenly
The day of his own death—

A short, pugnacious man, but honest and reliable.

Night fell and the mirror was empty for a while.
Then appeared, or half-appeared, Beatrice, my mother,
In the bed of her great age.
When she sleeps her human eye closes, and rests:
But her blind eye—the dead one—stares out
As if to say, "This is the forest primeval.
This is Death at last."

And I saw again the keepers of the graves
Moving among the shadows and the lights.

THE BRANCH

She could not keep her form.

Coming as a cat,
She became—forming, fainting, failing of form—
A woman loved. But then I could not,
Nor could she, hold her human

in evening light
Gravely drawing toward a truth.

I could not,
Despite the earnestness of long attempt,
Hold her human form, and she became a cat.
But even as a cat she labored at the countenance
I loved, which formed and was lost; and with
Enormous labor of her will, driven by love,
Formed again, and again faded and was lost
With a piteous cry;

but not before
I turned my back, and took her hand to lead
Into my house my bride.

The world became
Darker, the house lucid and dim like a mirror
Held to the Western sky. Matches not striking—
I could make nothing light. And then I felt
Her hand change to a soft claw.

Behind my back
The feeling of the claw become a hand,
And then her hand hopelessly a claw again,
Emptied my heart.

And I saw, as by another

Door forcing their way into the darkened house,
A crowd of men or boys, naked and in their strength,
One carrying a beautiful bare branch held high
With dew on it and light in the dew drops.

I commanded them to leave but they did not,
And grew more numerous

                              and the branch more
Coldly bright, and conquering.

STANZAS ON THE MOURNING OF NATIVITY

I

This June of inordinate rains what grows
Grows out of all measure.
The early season seems late so burdened
It is with leaves.
And the flow and lapse of streams, other years
Soft and slow,
Hews down *termini.* The mills dissolve
Into their race.
We are turned back—baffled, dispossessed—
By gigantic felicities
Of hedge, the long Spring grass, and trees.
Our sex has enlarged
The seeds of the earth. We have conceived
A child that must
Not live, because there is no dwelling in the wild
Fields of the world—
No tower, no law, no song, no animal—
He can inherit,
The woman sterile, the man of uncertain mind.

II

Such infants are like voices. The green trees
Are full of them.
They hold the sea islands. They have their nations
And their laws—their towers,
Songs, and animals. They are begotten too
Upon pictures, and also
In the cold false light of phosphorescence
On the bed of death—

At the moment of death when the visions come.
They are the hundred-armed,
The horned, the radiant, the too radiant children
That crowd the portals
And stairs, and from the infinite nursery of
The unborn look out,
Like light flashing from water as the wind rises
And the day cools—
And somewhere deep is the long curve of a dark arm
That comforts them,
When night seizes the sea islands and the nations.

III

In middle age he will not be quite whole.
This will be known
By his hesitation between man and woman
And by the terror
Of his sympathies, as light which is a sufferer
Shudders and grows pale
To be whatever thing on suffering earth
It falls upon.
For every real there is a hundred of his kind.
When he says "pain"
It is your pain. When he says "shores of ocean"
Black headlands
Receive the sea blow after shocking blow.
Of passions that have
No place in the world something is always born.
—Is there among
The burdened trees obscured by their own leafage
One oak that towers
Above and is the tower of solitary nurture?

IV

Now in his infancy, where swaddling light circles
And twists its chains
And everything that lives lives under the law
Of light spectacular,
Emperor of the unborn, he keeps the nest
Among the exploits
And suffering of the light—fugitive, voluptuary
With black all-focusing
Religious eyes, the father of his father
Of uncertain mind,
And mother of the sterile woman who
Has lost her road.
When he looks up, the stars leave signifying
And turn their fires;
When he looks down into the pouring mirror
Of the wimpled flood
The fire that passes through him from the stars
Burns in the water
Like a serpent crowned, and bites the root.

V

We are turned back. —The earth has overlain
The seeds of earth,
And will not wake. The rains drive down the nest
That was so high.
And thus begins the mourning of nativity:
The father grieves
In the meadows for his fantastic child.
The barren mother
Wanders the wet roads. And for its infant lord
The light weeps
Like an animal. The Summer will come,

The river slowly
Draw the ignorant flood into the sea.
Nothing will be
Added, and nothing taken away.
—We are alone.
In the world of the unborn his poem is
Very long.
In the world of the born, it is what you see.

FAUNESSE

Too weak, too too weak
To endure the presence of my own soul
Whom, in an afternoon, I tried to kill
For my peace.
And she wept soundlessly, without tears
(As deathless, in her patience, the soul grieves)
Asking me, "Why Why?
Why now, after love?" And I said to her,
"I am weary of my own soul,"
Thinking of

her darkened, unmistakable
Loving eyes,
The broken irises, and the masked lids
Scarred with beauty's marks by her poor, crazed mother's
Thumbs, as if for an evening without end
In the wild streets of Guatemala—
My own soul who is married to another,
As the soul is.
Let her go to her own kind

or to her
Solitude.
I have not the strength to live where my death is,
In the arms of my soul.
For surely I will meet her once again
In the unmade bed of my death which she will
Bring me, climbing the stair, with glittering eyes,
—Faunesse—
Bearing proudly the fatal knowledge love has
She comes to make perfect at the end:

A tropic plant with fat, magnetic leaves
From her eternal gardens

Wherein at a breath of its own mild airs
A flame breaks out, thorned flower that never dies.
My hands move toward my body—the hard hip,
The soft genital which has no good name.
I wish, now, to be alone with my hands
That are nearer to me.

THE PATH

The unborn. The unborn are what we were.

Among the unborn was one who saw the moon
In splendor rise. He was nearing the end
Of his life in the house of the unborn.
He knew it because the splendid moon had
Risen above the field. That was the sign
Of the end of one life.

                              —Then he harvested
The field in its season. Together with
The other harvesters he sang the song
That weeps for the grain.
Now the harvesters are a century gone
From the field

                    and the neighborhood grows older.

So many of the children have grown up
The path is less distinct year after year.
Soon it will be hard to find the short way
Through the field to school.

                              —Orpheus, Orpheus,
Master of losses, the children are come
And gone,

                    the harvesters.

                              And the trees return
With slow steps and the flowers with a skip,

And the grasses trailing long memories.

THE GOLDEN HOUSE

Once more my voice, tormented by the great
Hexameter of Venus and the grim
Rain of indivisible things,
Thunders in an angle of the cold hotel,
The tower no less desolate, the voice
No less a calling from cage to cage:
—There is void in all things.

                    What of the song?

We have the words of it, but not the song.
We have the need and the fear in which the song
Lies like a seed in the dry earth; but for us
The rain of song has never fallen, sweetening
And cleansing and quickening the seed of song.
The golden light that lights the house high up,
The green corner, the cornice that the light
Slicks gold, the northwest corner the low sun
Touches and judges not, I am now saying
To you it was the voice of her dream—
The bride of light dreaming in the house of light
Mantled in moss, the lavender, and flowering
Lichen, creeper, fennel, and watery thyme.

What of the song?

"Woman who has borne the man and the ecstasy
Of gods and men and given the world the light,
I call you munificent, milky, and high
Venus who have poured yourself into the sea
's bed and filled it so it bears great ships,
And the fame of your beauty into the earth
Under the quick wet kisses of the sky
And made fruit. Sweet you are sweet to raise

The bodies of us that we wake dazzled and see!
And the winds you make the flowing stair of
Your progress toward the standing house and evening
Arbor of your Summer throne.

                              Mother, for you
The earth lies down in flowers, and for you
The sky forgets the horror of the void
Above it and builds your house of light. There
Burns a solitary hearth and single
Candle in the one great room—until the father
Of dark limbs, the man who is himself the dark,
Covers your body as the shadows fall."

What of the song? What of the words of the song?

The grim rain thunders in its angle still,
The tower no less desolate, the voice
No less a calling from cage to cage.
If the house of the singer is not in order,
The words of the song are forgotten by morning.

—There is void in all things. And of themselves
They are without color and without a name.

THE GUARDIAN

After a while, things go on of themselves.

(There is no comfort, but there is a guardian.)

The guardian is a man and a woman.
He stands. She rests her body on his body
In an easy confident way.
She does not touch him with her hands

                                   which hold,
Instead, objects signifying mysteries.
— He also does not touch her with his hands.
Her left leg grips his waist and lies along
His thigh, opening her body to his sex.
Her right foot follows to the ground his left.
Beneath his penis struck into her cunt,
The smooth sack of heavy testicles hangs down.
And from the mountain altar of his hair
A human light descends on her. Her lips,
Curled back, display the long tooth of her love.

(The man and woman are in ecstasy.)

And this will be going on after my death,
And this will be going on after your death also.
But after a long time, all this will stop, flow
Back into the universe, cease form, cease
To be metal, become another thing,
Become nothing.

THE SPIRIT OF THE STAIR

Over and over the beauty of a flower
I saw just now at the head of the stair,
And am drawn out of myself. . . .

                         Therefore,
Whenever I consider journeying,
Only to you will I think of going away.
For you are one, my dear, to whom the thought
Must surely come, when you have passed a white
Flower on the stair and later it returns
Distinctly to your mind, that many have
Seen it the same and in many times;

And they are not in love, but they are not alone
In the great streams of the universe
Whom a white flower has drawn.

HIS NATION

Whatever the legislator Love devises must end
Now between us. For his world must have an end,
As thought must end, and action have an end
And not always be intending, and never still.

In justice, his scheme must be carried out quickly:
For the white, strengthless light of the late August moon
Is on the flowers, the nests washed from the willows.
Never is it once and for all the long water of love!

Take me, sister, where the rages are singers,
Walking in vivid garments—their beautiful
Bodies seen, and the light strong to see them in.

And there let him marry us in the justice of his nation.
In human truth the stream must form a pool, and stop.

THE SOUND OF A VOICE IS THE STORY
OF ITSELF

The sound of a voice, telling of its love
In clear words to the man or woman for whom
The love is love of that man or woman,
Is the story of itself
As the world is the story of itself
Told once to each mortal listener who
Hears it in a room alone—
How the sun shines, and moon adds its syllable,
And winds their emphasis, and rocks of earth
The full stop of difference which makes the sense
That claims him for the lineage of the world,
"Mortal listener!"

Mortal listener,
We have two breaths: the one that takes in
And is silent,
And the other one that gives, the outering
Breath and summoning of the world that tells
The story of the world.

The first breath is
Infant and mute, the feeding breath. It takes
The element which is the same in trees,
And on the lake, and in this room and the next
Room where the others are,
Into the body over the human tongue asleep.
The voice falls silent then, and body feeds
On the vital substance of the alien air,
And is alone, and suffers its death when full
For it can be no more.

But when the tongue
Awakes out of that lonely infancy

And turns to love,
A second breath that speaks makes of dead air,
And words common as air, a deathless summoning
Voice telling of its love
Which goes out at the punctual midnight
Of the body's dark, like a seed on the wind
Or a child leaving home,
And is never alone because it is
The sound of the world
Telling the story of itself in love
As to a woman bathing and making ready
Or a solitary man in a boat
Which the winds drive farther and farther
From the land.

And death will take us all, mortal listener,
At the sharp intaking of the deepest breath.
The sound of the voice falls silent; but then
Begins again telling the story of itself
In clear words: "This is love, which was your death,
And will be as you make it
Truth,
Between the one breath and the other breath."

THE BROOM

Corruption is the reciprocal to Generation: and they two,
are as Natures two terms or Boundaries.   —Bacon, *Sylva,* 328

First, on his neuter instrument the child
Sucking and blowing casts out simple threads;
And, then, the boy his trumpet, the girl her silver flute
Adorns as with webs the first light after rain.
Then, the man and woman in their prime utter
The vocal song, companion of the sun.
And their song goes with him, circling the world—
Cold at the pole—hot at the equator—
Gone up with the gull—with the highest clouds—
Where Phaeton screamed, for there was too much light.
So much light was darkness and he came to harm.

I have seen the bright nails scattered on the ground.

. . .

We sleep where we can. But the best thing is
A high bed in a white room with a picture
Of a dark seacoast, and the sea in storm.
The floor of the room must rest on the face
Of the earth and not be lower or higher
Than the common road. If there is dust,
Then sweep the room. Here is a worn straw
Broom to rid the vestiges of the gods.
Give up your little light, and let it be
Dark of the first darkness—the dark that was
Before the lonely, lonely transgression
Of the stars. And beware the unextinguishable
Interest of dreams. . . .

Between the head and foot of the high bed
The grim genital of the world repeats

In you and says its say: The body is
The place of final claims.

                              Until the slow
Light fills—
To whatever honor—by whatever servile hand—
The long, Lethean chalice of the day.

                    •   •   •

Lying late like a false watchman
In bed at the hour when vigilance would
Be rewarded on the ramparts, and a thin
Snow falling like the pollen of desolate
Ashen flowers blowing above in the dark
Lunar garden of the winter sky at noon—
My death appeared to me high up in the air
Of a white room,
Like a snarled hank of somebody's black hair
—And more and more often now appears.

It convinces me I have seen my soul.

                              —Watchman,
As you walk the ramparts with the cold sift
Of the snow charging the shoulders of your coat,
Have you seen your death-soul as I have mine?

                    •   •   •

Whenas the brightest planet hunts the moon
As, now, night after night I see it do,
Sense falls like thin snow on broken ground:
If I loved you but not of your body,
I did not love you. But I loved you

And I love you.

THE VOICE

It is good to hear the voice of a man.

It is good to hear the voice of a woman.

The voice of a man or the voice of a woman
Is truth enough to justify our death.

There are other voices but they do not
Justify, as the sea is a great voice.

The voice of a woman says the name of a man.
"Allen," she says, "my brother, and my love."

(It is good to hear the voice of a woman.)

The voice of a man says the name of a woman.
"Luce," he says, "my sister, and my love."

(It is good to hear the voice of a man.)

The voice of a man and a woman is one voice.

QUIES, *OR REST*

A woman goes from room to room. She extinguishes
One light in each room. Darkness follows her
And in the last room she is overtaken.
Then, she mounts the dark stair confidently
And enters the room she sleeps in, and lies
Down in the dark, where a man in the dark wakes
A little and covers her with his arm.

New Directions Paperbooks—A Partial Listing

For complete listing request complete catalog from
New Directions, 80 Eighth Avenue, New York 10011   † Bilingual